SUPER SIMPLE
ZOO
CRITTER CRAFTS

Fun and Easy Animal Crafts

Sammy Bosch

Consulting Editor, Diane Craig, M.A./Reading Specialist

Super Sandcastle

An Imprint of Abdo Publishing
abdopublishing.com

abdopublishing.com

Published by Abdo Publishing, a division of ABDO, PO Box 398166, Minneapolis, Minnesota 55439. Copyright © 2017 by Abdo Consulting Group, Inc. International copyrights reserved in all countries. No part of this book may be reproduced in any form without written permission from the publisher. Super SandCastle™ is a trademark and logo of Abdo Publishing.

Printed in the United States of America, North Mankato, Minnesota
062016
092016

Editor: Liz Salzmann
Content Developer: Nancy Tuminelly
Craft Production: Frankie Tuminelly
Cover and Interior Design and Production: Colleen Dolphin, Mighty Media, Inc.
Photo Credits: LMspencer/Shutterstock; Mighty Media, Inc.; Shutterstock
The following manufacturers/names appearing in this book are trademarks:
Paper Mate®, Polymark®, SchoolWorks®, Sharpie®, Styrofoam™

Library of Congress Cataloging-in-Publication Data
Names: Bosch, Sammy, author.
Title: Super simple zoo critter crafts : fun and easy animal crafts / by Sammy Bosch ; consulting editor, Diane Craig, M.A./reading specialist.
Other titles: Zoo critter crafts
Description: Minneapolis, Minnesota : ABDO Publishing, [2017] | Series: Super simple critter crafts
Identifiers: LCCN 2016001348 (print) | LCCN 2016002514 (ebook) | ISBN 9781680781656 (print) | ISBN 9781680776089 (ebook)
Subjects: LCSH: Handicraft--Juvenile literature. | Zoo animals--Juvenile literature.
Classification: LCC TT160 .B758 2017 (print) | LCC TT160 (ebook) | DDC 745.59--dc23
LC record available at http://lccn.loc.gov/2016001348

Super SandCastle™ books are created by a team of professional educators, reading specialists, and content developers around five essential components—phonemic awareness, phonics, vocabulary, text comprehension, and fluency—to assist young readers as they develop reading skills and strategies and increase their general knowledge. All books are written, reviewed, and leveled for guided reading and early reading intervention programs for use in shared, guided, and independent reading and writing activities to support a balanced approach to literacy instruction.

TO ADULT HELPERS

The craft projects in this series are fun and simple. There are just a few things to remember to keep kids safe. Some projects require the use of sharp or hot objects. Also, kids may be using messy materials such as glue or paint. Make sure they protect their clothes and work surfaces. Review the projects before starting, and be ready to assist when necessary.

KEY SYMBOL

Watch for this warning symbol in this book. Here is what it means.

🔥 HOT!
You will be working with something hot. Get help from an adult!

CONTENTS

ZOO CRITTERS

Animals from all over the world live in zoos! Many of these animals are **endangered**. Zoos can protect these animals.

Zoo critters are fun to watch. They are wild animals that can't live in people's homes. But you can make your own zoo! Try these projects and learn about zoos and zoo animals.

GET TO KNOW ZOO ANIMALS!

FUN FACTS ABOUT YOUR FAVORITE ZOO ANIMALS

ELEPHANTS

There are two **species** of elephants. They are African elephants and Asian elephants.

PENGUINS

Penguins are birds, but they cannot fly. They are great swimmers. They use their wings like flippers.

TIGERS

Tigers are the largest cats. Their stripes help them **blend** in to their surroundings.

GIRAFFES

Giraffes are the tallest land animals. They can be 18 feet (5.5 m) tall. Their tongues can be 1½ feet (0.5 m) long!

POLAR BEARS

Polar bears weigh 700 to 1,600 pounds (300 to 725 kg). They eat mainly seals.

PEAFOWL

A male peafowl is a peacock. Females are peahens. Only peacocks have colorful tails.

WOLVES

Wolves live in packs. They form a **hierarchy**. Usually only the top male and female in a pack have babies.

GORILLAS

Gorillas are very smart. Koko the gorilla learned sign language. She knows more than 1,000 signs.

ALL ABOUT ZOOS

Learn about zoos and nature reserves

SAN DIEGO ZOO

The San Diego Zoo was the first zoo to use natural, cageless **habitats**. More than 3,700 animals live there.

nature reserves

Nature reserves are large areas where the animals and plants are protected. People can go on **safari** in nature reserves. They take pictures of the animals there.

MATERIALS

Here are some of the things you'll need to do the projects.

acrylic paint

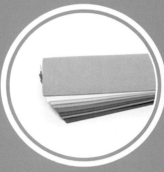

brown or black sock

cellophane frill toothpicks

colored paper

craft feathers

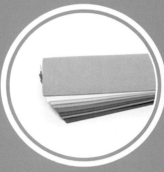

craft foam

craft sticks

dry beans

felt

googly eyes

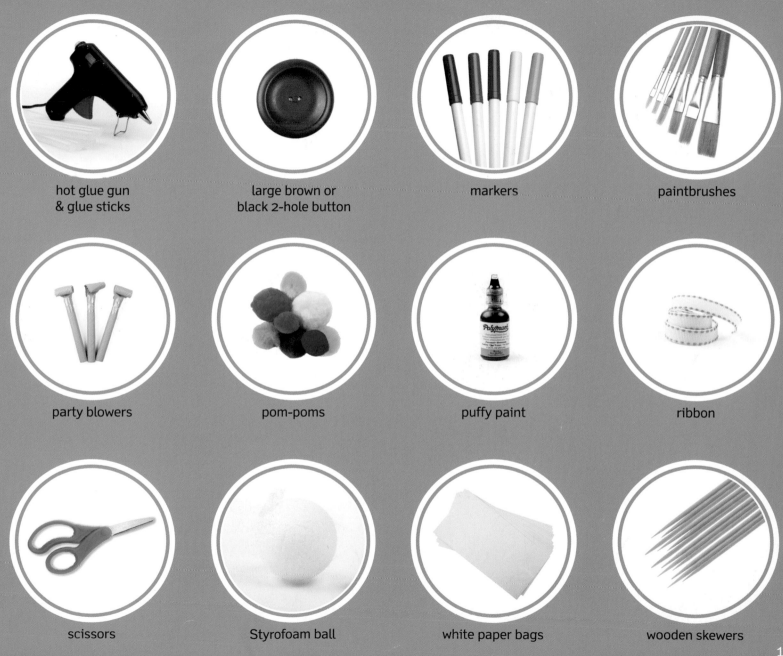

hot glue gun
& glue sticks

large brown or
black 2-hole button

markers

paintbrushes

party blowers

pom-poms

puffy paint

ribbon

scissors

Styrofoam ball

white paper bags

wooden skewers

11

TRUMPETING ELEPHANTS

Celebrate elephants with these party blowers!

MATERIALS

craft foam	scissors	googly eyes
black marker	craft glue	party blowers
ruler		

1. Draw two 2½-inch (6.5 cm) circles on craft foam. Cut out the circles. Cut one circle in half.

2. The half-circles are the ears. Glue them on each side of the full circle. The round edges should stick out. Glue two googly eyes between the ears.

3. Draw a rectangle on craft foam. Make it 5½ by 3 inches (14 by 8 cm). Cut out the rectangle. Draw a small square in the center of each end. Cut out the squares. This is the body and legs.

4. Punch a hole near each square cutout on the body. Punch a hole below the googly eyes. Trim around the holes as needed so a party blower can fit through them.

5. Push the party blower through the hole in the head. Then push it through the holes in the body.

6. Repeat steps 1 through 5 to make more elephants.

THESE PENGUINS WILL
MARCH INTO YOUR HEART!

MATERIALS

Styrofoam ball	skewer	yellow & black craft foam
plastic knife	black acrylic paint	scissors
newspaper	paintbrush	2 googly eyes
marker	pencil	craft glue

1. Cut a slice from the side of the ball so it will sit flat.

2. Cover your work surface with newspaper. Hold the ball with the flat side toward you. Starting at the base of the flat edge, draw a half circle on the ball. This is the penguin's stomach.

3. Stick a skewer into the flat side of the ball. Paint everywhere except the stomach and flat side black. Hold onto the skewer to keep paint off your fingers. Let the paint dry.

(continued on next page)

4 Draw wings on black craft foam. Make them about as long as the ball is wide. Cut them out.

5 Draw feet and a beak on yellow foam. Cut them out.

6 Glue the googly eyes above the stomach.

16

7. Glue the beak under the eyes.

8. Glue the feet to the bottom of the penguin. Place them right next to each other.

9. Glue the wings on the sides of the body. They should hang down past the feet slightly. Let the glue dry.

TINY TIGER PUPPET

THIS CUDDLY KITTY WILL
FOLLOW YOU EVERYWHERE!

MATERIALS

orange & pink felt · pencil · craft glue

ruler · ribbon · puffy paint

scissors

1   Cut two rectangles out of orange felt. Make each one 1½ inches (4 cm) wide and as long as your finger.

2   Cut the ears and top of the head out of one rectangle. Trace the shape on the other rectangle. Cut it out.

3   Cut two 2½-inch (6.5 cm) pieces of ribbon. Fold them in half. Glue the ends together. These are the tiger's arms.

4   Put glue along the sides and top of one rectangle. Don't put glue on the straight end. Lay the arms on the glue. Put glue on the arms. Press the second rectangle on top. Make sure the edges line up.

5   Draw triangles on the body with puffy paint. Color in the top of the head between the ears.

6   Cut a small triangle out of pink felt. Glue it on the face for the nose. Draw eyes and a mouth with puffy paint. Let the paint and glue dry.

19

TALL TUBE GIRAFFE

make a
LONG-NECKED
FRIEND!

MATERIALS

3 toilet paper tubes

scissors

pencil

craft glue

paper towel tube

ruler

newspaper

yellow & brown acrylic paint

paintbrush

brown yarn

2 cellophane frill toothpicks

2 googly eyes

1 Cut a toilet paper tube open. Flatten the cardboard. Draw the **profile** of a giraffe head on half of it. Draw lines from the head to the edge of the cardboard, creating a flap. Cut out the head, including the flap.

2 Trace the shape on the other half of the cardboard. Cut out the second head shape. Put glue on one head shape. Do not put glue on the flap. Press the second head shape on top. Make sure the edges line up. Let the glue dry.

3 Measure 4 inches (10 cm) from one end of the paper towel tube. Cut a triangle in the side of the tube.

4 Bend the tube so that the long end sticks up. It is the giraffe's neck. The short end is the body.

(continued on next page)

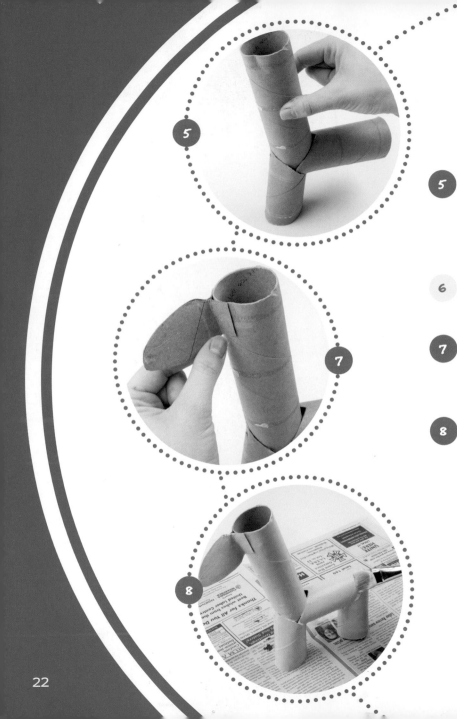

5 Cut one end of each toilet paper tube off at an angle. Glue the corner of the paper towel tube into one of the toilet paper tubes.

6 Glue the back of the body into the other toilet paper tube.

7 Separate the flaps on the head. Glue them to the top of the neck. Let the glue dry.

8 Cover your work surface with newspaper. Paint the giraffe yellow.

9   Cut about 20 pieces of yarn. Make them each about 2 inches (5 cm) long. Put a line of glue down the back of the giraffe's neck. Place the pieces of yarn across the glue.

10 Paint brown spots on the giraffe.

11 Paint the frilly end of each toothpick brown. Glue the toothpicks inside the neck above the head. These are the giraffe's **ossicones**.

12 Glue a googly eye to each side of the head.

13 Cut a 3-inch (8 cm) piece of yarn for the tail. Glue it to the back end of the giraffe.

THIS GORILLA WILL GREET YOU WITH A SMILE!

24

MATERIALS 🔥

brown or black sock	large brown or black	black felt
cotton balls	2-hole button	2 black pom-poms
dry beans	hot glue gun	2 googly eyes
scissors	& glue sticks	black puffy paint

1 Fill the sock halfway with cotton balls. Put three handfuls of beans on top of the cotton balls. Tie the sock in a knot. Cut off the extra sock. The knot is the bottom of the gorilla.

2 Glue the button near the top of the sock. This is the face. The holes are the **nostrils**.

3 Cut two arm shapes out of black felt. They should be about as long as the sock is high.

4 Glue the arms on each side of the head. Glue a black pom-pom to the end of each arm for hands.

5 Glue the googly eyes to the button above the nostrils. Draw a mouth with puffy paint.

PLUSH POLAR BEAR

THIS CRITTER IS
"un-BEARABLY" ADORABLE!

MATERIALS 🔥

2 white paper bags	4 toilet paper tubes	12 small black pom-poms
newspaper	cotton balls	1 large black pom-pom
large rubber band	hot glue gun & glue sticks	2 googly eyes

1. Stuff both white bags with **crumpled** newspaper. Stuff one bag three-fourths full. It is the bear's body. Stuff the other bag one-third full. This is the head.

2. Put the opening of the head bag over the opening of the body. Wrap the rubber band around the **overlapped** bags to form the neck.

3. Glue cotton balls all over the toilet paper tubes. They are the legs. Glue three small black pom-poms to the end of each leg for claws.

4. Glue the legs to the body.

5. Glue cotton balls all over the rest of the bear's body.

6. Glue two cotton balls to the head for ears. Glue the large black pom-pom on the face for the nose. Glue the googly eyes above the nose. Let the glue dry.

HOWLING WOLF PUPPET

HOWL TO THE MOON IN YOUR ROOM!

MATERIALS

dark brown paper	pencil	2 googly eyes
ruler	light brown paper	black pom-pom
scissors	craft glue	craft stick

1. Cut a 5-inch (13 cm) square piece of dark brown paper. Draw a wolf face on it. Cut it out.

2. Draw rounded triangles out of dark brown paper for ears. Cut them out. Cut two smaller triangles out of light brown paper. Glue them to the middle of the ears.

3. Draw two **kidney-bean** shapes on light brown paper. Make them about as long as the wolf's face. Cut them out. Glue them to the face.

4. Glue the googly eyes to the tops of the kidney-bean cutouts. Glue the ears to the back of the head.

5. Glue a black pom-pom to the bottom of the head for the nose.

6. Glue the craft stick to the back of the head. Use it to hold your puppet.

29

A PRETTY PEACOCK
THAT DAZZLES!

MATERIALS 🔥

newspaper	marker	clear tape
paper plate	scissors	blue & green craft feathers
blue watercolor paint	craft glue	
paintbrush	2 googly eyes	hot glue gun & glue sticks
blue & orange paper	4 blue frill toothpicks	

1 Cover your work surface with newspaper. Paint the paper plate with blue watercolor paint. Let the paint dry.

2 Draw a bowling pin shape on blue paper. Make it about two-thirds as tall as the plate is wide. Cut it out. This is the peacock's head and body.

3 Draw a beak on the orange paper and cut it out. Glue the beak to the face. Glue the googly eyes above the beak.

4 Tape the toothpicks to the back of the head.

5 Hot glue the feathers around the edge of the plate. **Alternate** colors. Glue the body in the middle over the ends of the feathers.

31

GLOSSARY

alternate – to change back and forth from one to the other.

blend – to match the surrounding environment.

crumple – to crush or bend something out of shape.

endangered – having few left in the world.

habitat – the area or environment where a person or animal usually lives.

hierarchy – a way of organizing a group into different ranks or levels of importance.

kidney bean – an edible seed that is usually dark red.

nostril – an opening in the nose.

ossicone – a hornlike bump on the heads of some animals including giraffes and okapis.

overlap – to lie partly on top of something.

profile – the shape of something as seen from the side.

safari – a trip taken to see large wild animals, especially in Africa.

species – a group of related living beings.